Science and Technology
Food Technology

Neil Morris

Chicago, Illinois

www.heinemannraintree.com
Visit our website to find out
more information about
Heinemann-Raintree books.

To order:

☎ Phone 888-454-2279

💻 Visit www.heinemannraintree.com
to browse our catalog and order online.

Edited by Andrew Farrow, Adam Miller, and Diyan Leake
Designed by Victoria Allen
Original illustrations © Capstone Global Library Ltd 2012
Illustrated by Oxford Designers & Ilustrators
Picture research by Elizabeth Alexander
Originated by Capstone Global Library Ltd
Printed and bound in China by CTPS

15 14 13 12 11
10 9 8 7 6 5 4 3 2 1

Library of Congress Cataloging-in-Publication Data
Morris, Neil, 1946-
    Food technology / Neil Morris.
        p. cm.—(Sci-hi: science and technology)
    Includes bibliographical references and index.
    ISBN 978-1-4109-4274-6 (hc)—ISBN 978-1-4109-4283-8
(pb) 1. Food industry and trade—Juvenile literature. 2.
Nutrition—Juvenile literature. I. Title.
    TP370.3.M67 2012
    664—dc22   2010054329

Acknowledgments
The author and publishers are grateful to the following
for permission to reproduce copyright material: Alamy
pp. **12** (© H. Mark Weidman Photography), **14**
(© Spazio Foto Mereghetti), **16** (© Marco Regalia),
24 (© Phototake Inc.), **26** (© keith morris), **29** (© Neil
Setchfield), **32** (© Image Source), **36** (© David R. Frazier
Photolibrary, Inc.), **38** (© BlueMoon Stock); Corbis pp. **6**
(© Peet Simard), **17** (© Ed Darack/Science Faction), **19**
top (© Peter Ginter/Science Faction), **28** (© Envision),
40 (© Danny Lehman); Corbis Sygma p. **31** (© Pitchal
Frederic); Getty Images pp. **10** (Michael Rosenfeld/
Stone), **19** bottom (Gary Ombler/ Dorling Kindersley),
25 (Nick White/Photodisc); NASA p. **15**; Photolibrary
pp. **5** (Javier Larrea), **27** (Huw Jones); Science Photo
Library pp. **9** (Thierry Berrod, Mona Lisa Production);
Shutterstock pp. **4** (© VR Photos), **8** (© Borodaev), **11**
(© jordache), **30** (© Nayashkova Olga), **20** (© Golden
Pixels LLC), **21** (© Joe Gough), **23** (© Bragin Alexey), **22**
(© Thomas Zobl), **34** (© Kharidehal Abhirama Ashwin),
35 bottom (© VIPDesignUSA), **39** (© Goodluz), **13**
(© Roman Sigaev), **35** top (© Wire_man), **contents
page** top (© Roman Sigaev), **contents page** bottom
(© Wire_man), **all background and design features**.

Main cover photograph of packaging cold cuts
reproduced with permission of Corbis (© Russ
Schleipman); inset cover photograph of soft drink
bubble reproduced with permission of shutterstock
(© 2jenn).

The publisher would like to thank literary consultant
Nancy Harris and content consultant Suzy Gazlay for
their assistance in the preparation of this book.

Every effort has been made to contact copyright holders
of material reproduced in this book. Any omissions will
be rectified in subsequent printings if notice is given to
the publisher.

Contents

What are vitamins?

Turn to page 8 to find out!

When were pulls tabs first used?

Find out on page 35!

Some words are shown in bold, **like this**. These words are explained in the glossary. You will find important information and definitions underlined, <u>like this</u>.

WHAT IS FOOD?

Food gives us the **energy** (strength) we need for everything we do. We cannot live without food. It helps us think, work, and run around. Eating the right amount of good food keeps us healthy. In food technology, we study how good food products are made. There are many processes involved. We find out how people grow, process, package, and sell food products. We also learn how to prepare and cook food that is healthy, safe, and good to eat.

Knowledge of food technology helps these cooks produce safe, healthy meals in their restaurant.

THE SCIENCE OF FOOD

In the kitchen, cooks put **ingredients** (parts of a mixture) together to make tasty dishes and meals. In the **laboratory** (a place where scientists work), food scientists combine their ingredients to make products for people to buy. Cooks and scientists are all involved in food technology.

MEASURING FOOD ENERGY

We measure the energy we get from food in units called **calories**. People trying to lose weight often see calories as a bad thing. But we all need calories every day—just not too many of them. One calorie is a tiny amount of energy, so scientists count in thousands of calories, called **kilocalories (kcal)**. But to confuse things, most people call these bigger units "calories." Food scientists also use a unit called a **kilojoule (kJ)**, which is about the same amount as one quarter of a kilocalorie.

LOUIS PASTEUR (1822–1895)

In 1864 the French scientist Louis Pasteur discovered that heat destroys the **bacteria** (tiny living things) that make food and drink go bad. This was successful early food technology. Today, milk is still made safer by heating it to 72 degrees Celsius (°C), or 162 degrees Fahrenheit (°F), for 15 seconds. The heating is called **pasteurization**, after Pasteur.

Nutrients

The natural chemicals in food that help us live are called **nutrients**. The nutrients that we need in large amounts are called **macronutrients**. The nutrients that we need in much smaller amounts are called **micronutrients**. **Carbohydrates**, **proteins**, and **fats** make up the macronutrients.

Simple sugars and complex starches

Carbohydrates form our most important source of energy. There are two main types of carbohydrate. They are called simple sugars and complex starches. These are changed into a substance called **glucose** when we eat them. Glucose provides us with energy.

Food scientists divide sugars into these main groups:

- *Glucose*: Found in fruits and honey
- *Fructose*: Found in fruits and vegetables
- *Lactose*: Found in milk and dairy products
- *Sucrose*: Found in sugar beet and sugar cane, which is used to make table sug

Starches are made up of glucose units joined together. They are found in cereals (such as rice and wheat) and potatoes.

The flour in bread is made by grinding the grains (or seeds) of cereals such as wheat.

WHICH MACRONUTRIENTS ARE IN THE FOOD WE EAT?

	Carbohydrate	Protein	Fat
Apple	100 %	0 %	0 %
Brown rice	81 %	10 %	9 %
Chicken breast	0 %	73 %	27 %
Eggs	1 %	38 %	61 %
Lentils	67 %	30 %	3 %
Whole wheat bread	74 %	12 %	14 %

Bodybuilders

Protein helps the body grow and repair itself. There are lots of proteins in:

- red meat, such as beef, lamb, and pork
- poultry, such as chicken
- fish
- **pulses** (edible seeds of crops like peas, beans, and lentils), nuts, and seeds.

Good and bad fats

Fats are a source of energy that also help the body take in healthy substances called **vitamins** (see box on page 8). People sometimes think that fats are bad for them. That is because the types called **saturated fats**, found in meat, can increase the risk of heart disease. But **unsaturated fats**, such as vegetable oils, can be called "good" fats. Experts think that chemicals called fatty acids in oily fish help reduce the risk of heart disease.

VITAMINS

Vitamins are micronutrients. They are chemicals that help us live and grow. Vitamins are usually known by letter codes rather than their scientific names. Our bodies cannot store some vitamins, such as vitamin B and vitamin C. We need a constant supply of these vitamins from the food we eat.

Fruits are a good source of vitamins and other nutrients. Large markets offer many different kinds of fruit, depending on the season.

Vitamin	Chemical name	Good food sources
A	Retinol	Carrots, dairy products
B_1	Thiamin	Nuts, vegetables, whole grains
B_9	Folic acid	Fruits, leafy green vegetables
B_{12}	Cobalamin	Eggs, fish, meat, poultry
C	Ascorbic acid	Citrus fruit, broccoli
D	Calciferol	Margarine, oily fish

Minerals

We also need tiny quantities of about 15 **minerals**, which are found naturally in the ground. Essential minerals are calcium, iron, magnesium, phosphorus, potassium, sodium, and sulfur.

Food groups

We can put foods into five main groups:

- *Bread, cereal grains, and potatoes*: These starchy foods are full of carbohydrates and **fiber** (a plant material needed for health). They should make up about one-third of the food we eat.

- *Fruits and vegetables*: These contain carbohydrates, vitamins, and fiber. We should eat at least five portions every day.

- *Milk and dairy products*: These are a good source of protein, vitamins, and calcium. We should eat moderate amounts.

- *Meat, fish, beans, nuts, and pulses*: These contain lots of protein. Most people get as much protein as they need from eating a normal diet.

- *Fats and sugar*: These include oils, cookies, cakes, chips, and soda. We need to eat some good fats, but we should not eat too many bad fats or sugary foods.

FLAVOROLOGY

Would you like to be a flavor scientist, known as a flavorologist? You would get to taste a lot of different foods. The job involves testing out how different food chemicals mix with each other. For example, proteins, carbohydrates, and fats react differently with chemicals that give flavor or smell. So, scientists work hard to find ways to make low-fat foods as full of flavor as higher-fat varieties.

FOOD PRODUCTION

Food companies produce food in a complex process that has many different stages. It begins with growing crops and raising animals to provide high-quality ingredients. The next stage is the **manufacturing** process, when food is made. The packaged products are then transported to stores, such as supermarkets.

Food-making processes

There are three different production processes:

- *Single-item production:* This means making a single product. This is usually for a luxury food item such as a cake.
- *Batch production*: This means making a set number of the same product.
- *Continuous-flow production*: This is a form of **mass production** (making many of the same thing) that goes on nonstop.

Bakery workers check the bread as it comes out of the oven.

In this process, tarts are filled with jam as they pass underneath nozzles.

DIFFERENT PROCESSES FOR DIFFERENT PRODUCTS

Here are some examples of foods produced by the different systems. Can you think of some more?

• Single-item production includes cakes, especially for birthdays. This is something you could design yourself. Individual birthday boys and girls might have special wishes for shape, size, and ingredients.

• Batch production includes bread, with different kinds of loaf baked in each batch.

• Continuous-flow production includes big-selling products, such as frozen pizza (see page 30).

CAD AND CAM

• Computer-aided design (CAD) allows food designers and manufacturers to test packages and products before spending a lot of money mass-producing them.

• Computer-aided manufacture (CAM) allows manufacturers to control and check every stage of the manufacturing process. They can check amounts of ingredients, speeds of conveyor belts (machines that move things along), and oven temperatures. Large bakeries use one basic CAM system to produce different types of bread. The computer changes the amount of ingredients for each batch.

Industrial equipment

Large-scale food manufacturing equipment is similar to ordinary kitchen utensils. But it is much bigger and stronger.

Equipment	Use
Centrifuge	Spins ingredients to separate liquids from solids
Deck oven	Contains heated chambers, one above the other, each separately controlled
Depositor	Funnel, nozzle, or tube that fills containers with a measured amount
Hopper	Large, funnel-shaped container used to give out ingredients
Mandolin	Slices ingredients thinly and evenly
Mixer	Floor-standing machine for mixing large quantities of ingredients
Tunnel oven	A connected series of heated chambers that a conveyor belt carries food through
Vat	Large container for storing and cooking

This mixing machine helps to make smooth chocolate in a large vat.

Watery production

Food production uses up enormous amounts of a precious resource—water. It takes these amounts of water to produce these foods:

To make …	… the water needed is:
1 slice of bread from a standard size loaf	40 liters (11 gallons)
1 50-gram (about 2-ounce) bag of chips*	46 liters (12 gallons)
1 can of cola	200 liters (53 gallons)
1 kilogram (2.2 pounds) of cheese	5,000 liters (1,320 gallons)

* The original potatoes are 80 percent water. After using all that water, mainly for washing the potatoes, the fried and dried chips have a water content of just 2 percent.

WHY IS SODA FIZZY?

The fizz in a can or bottle of soda is bubbles of gas. If you open a screw-top bottle slowly and carefully, you will see the bubbles rush to the surface. The gas is called **carbon dioxide**. **Manufacturers** (people who make the products) put the gas into the drink under pressure when they bottle it. The gas dissolves into the liquid. When you open the bottle, the pressure is released, and the carbon dioxide turns back into gas. This bubbles up and makes a hissing sound as it reaches the air.

QUALITY CONTROL

Food manufacturers have to make sure that their products are of high quality. <u>Shoppers will only buy from companies if they think their food is safe</u>. So, it is important for manufacturers to have an effective control system, which carefully checks their procedures. Some of the quality checks are controlled by computer.

This cheese-maker is tapping a cheese with a hammer. He can tell from the sound what the cheese is like inside.

Hazard analysis

Manufacturers use **hazard analysis** to identify potential dangers. There are three kinds of danger to food production:

- biological hazards, such as harmful bacteria
- chemical hazards, such as cleaning fluids or machine oil getting into food (called **contamination**)
- physical hazards, such as pieces of glass or workers' hair entering food.

In the Hazard Analysis Critical Control Points (HACCP) system, checks are made at the points where dangers are most likely to occur. This system is very successful for quality control.

IDEAS FROM SPACE

HACCP was first used in the 1960s, when the U.S. space agency NASA asked a company to produce safe food for its astronauts. It was very important that astronauts remained healthy, and they did not want any pieces of food floating around their spaceship. So, NASA asked for bite-sized foods that were free of harmful bacteria and crumbs. The food company set up the first HACCP system to make sure their space food was perfectly safe.

These people working on the International Space Station are sharing a meal in space.

STOPPING FOOD POISONING

In 1996 there was an outbreak of food poisoning in Scotland. Nearly 500 people got sick, and 17 died. The cause was found to be contamination of cooked meat caused by bacteria called *E. coli.* Following an investigation, the HACCP system was adopted throughout the whole British food industry. The United Nations Food and Agriculture Organization agreed that it was essential to bring in a food safety system like this.

PRESERVING FOOD

In ancient times the most popular methods of **preserving** food (keeping it from spoiling) were drying, salting, and smoking. All these methods remove water from food to stop or slow the spread of harmful **microorganisms** (tiny living things such as bacteria).

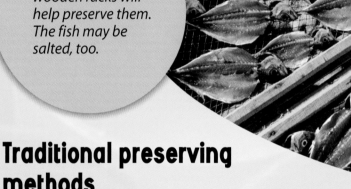

Drying fish on these wooden racks will help preserve them. The fish may be salted, too.

Traditional preserving methods

Other traditional preserving methods include:

- *Fermenting*: Using **yeast** (a kind of microorganism) or bacteria to produce chemicals called acids and alcohols
- *Jamming*: Boiling in a sugar mixture
- *Pickling*: Covering food with an **acid solution**, such as vinegar.

Canning was introduced in the 1800s, for preserving meats, fruits, and vegetables. Freezing came in a century later. Freezing is effective because the low temperature in a freezer kills the microorganisms that cause food to go bad.

Cans of peeled tomatoes pass along a production line in a canning factory.

BRIGHT IDEAS: BOTTLING AND FREEZING

In the early 1800s, the French candy-maker Nicolas Appert developed a way to preserve fruits, vegetables, and soups in glass jars. He used cork stoppers reinforced (strengthened) with wire and sealing wax. Then he placed the sealed jars in boiling water for a few hours.

In 1929 the U.S. businessman Clarence Birdseye started selling quick-frozen fish. He had seen on trips to Canada how people froze food to make it last through the winter. His Birds Eye Foods Company is still famous for its frozen fish and vegetables.

Heat and radiation

The **Ultra Heat Treatment (UHT)** process heats milk to more than 135 °C (275 °F) for just one second. An unopened carton of UHT milk can last for up to six months. Another process, called **irradiation**, bombards food with a kind of light called gamma rays. These rays, or beams, kill microorganisms. If a food has undergone one of these processes, it is shown on the label.

Additives

Chemicals called **additives** are used to improve the qualities of processed foods, such as:

- preserving (increasing the shelf-life of the product)
- changing texture (the way the food feels in the mouth), such as making food smoother
- improving color, taste, or smell.

Some people are sensitive to certain additives, so they need to know what is in their food. In most countries, all additives have to be listed on food labels.

Genetic Modification— Yes or No?

Genetic modification (GM) means changing an animal's or a plant's **genes**. Genes are the basic units that pass characteristics, such as size and color, from one generation to the next. GM can be used to make crops more useful. But many people who are concerned about the environment (called **environmentalists**) are against it.

Arguments for and against GM

For—GM foods could …	Against—GM foods could …
✓ build up resistance to (the ability to fight) pests	✗ spread to non-GM crops and wipe them out
✓ help the **developing world** (poorer parts of the world) by increasing harvests	✗ leave farmers in the hands of giant companies that control GM seeds
✓ lower food costs by increasing the amount each plant produces	✗ reduce biodiversity (the world's wide range of plants and animals)
✓ benefit health by being enriched with nutrients	✗ have health risks that we will only discover when it is too late
✓ improve taste and shelf life.	✗ have consequences that people don't know about or haven't thought of yet.

What do you think? Should people produce GM foods or not? Use the arguments above to make and explain your decision.

Vegetarian cheese

Cheese is traditionally made using rennet, which comes from calves' stomachs. Rennet naturally separates milk into lumps. In the 1980s scientists found a way to create the substance that makes rennet work. They did this by taking genes from rennet and putting them into microorganisms. The resulting cheese is not labeled GM, because the microorganisms are not actually part of the cheese. And vegetarians can eat it, because it contains no material from animals.

If these cheese-makers do not use rennet, the cheese can be labeled as suitable for vegetarians.

Organic production

A food is labeled "organic" if it has been produced without the use of pesticides (chemicals used to kill pests, or insects) or human-made fertilizers (chemicals that help plants grow). Environmentalists say that organic farming is much better for the land. Also, by eating organic foods, we are less likely to be eating chemicals. But is organic food better for you? Some scientific studies show that organic food is safer and more nutritious, while others find no difference.

COOKING TECHNIQUES

Food production in the home is similar to food processing in factories. The difference is that things are done on a much smaller scale at home.

Food technology at home includes a number of processes:

- storing raw food
- preparing a range of ingredients (cutting, grindi weighing, and so on)
- combining ingredients
- shaping foods
- cooking and cooling
- storing cooked food safely and **hygienically** (cleanly).

This cook is carefully cutting raw fish into thin slices.

ANCIENT METHODS

The ancient Greeks and Romans wrote about the \ prepared food. A wealthy Roman merchant named Gavius Apicius was an expert on fine food and wine during the 1st century CE. Historians believe he wrote a book of 500 Roman recipes called *De re coquinaria* ("On the Subject of Cookery"). A century later, a Greek cook named Athenaeus wrote a book on food. It follows a conversation between two men enjoying a feast.

Combining ingredients

Food scientists, chefs in restaurants, and cooks at home use the same basic ingredients to make their dishes. Ingredients react with each other in different ways, depending on their chemical makeup. Here are some of the basic combining processes.

Binding	Causing ingredients to stick together—for example, using egg in a cookie dough
Breading	Coating food with an ingredient like bread crumbs
Enriching	Adding ingredients such as vitamins or minerals to improve the **nutritional** quality of food
Flavoring	Adding ingredients to change flavor, such as herbs and spices, or sugar for sweetening
Setting	Using ingredients to make foods firm, such as gelatin for some desserts
Shortening	Using fats, such as lard or margarine, to make pastries less stretchy and more crumbly
Stabilizing	Adding ingredients, such as eggs and flour, to help food keep its structure.

This cod fish was coated in bread crumbs before it was cooked.

FLAVORING CHIPS

From 1920 to 1960, bags of chips were sold with a dash of salt. Then, manufacturers found that people wanted different flavor, such as cheese or sour cream and onion. The flavor comes from powdered seasoning, which is sprayed onto the chips just after frying. The seasoning flavors are originally made from the real food—cheese, onion, salt, and so on.

Emulsion, foam, or gel?

There are different kinds of mixtures in cooking, depending on how ingredients react with each other:

- A **solution** is formed when one ingredient dissolves in another. Syrup is a solution of sugar dissolved in water.

- An **emulsion** is a mixture of two liquids that will not form a solution. The liquids (such as oil and vinegar) need a substance called an emulsifier (such as the lecithin in egg yolk) to stop them from separating again.

- A foam forms when air mixes with a liquid (such as whipped cream or meringue)

- A gel is a semi-solid mixture (such as jelly). It is made of a small amount of solid (gelatin) in liquid (water).

- In a **suspension**, a solid (such as flour) is held in a liquid (such as milk). The solid does not dissolve and may sink if it not stirred (for example, when making cheese sauce).

BATTERY-CAGE OR CAGE-FREE EGGS?

Battery hens are kept in cages. Cage-free eggs are produced by hens that are kept in sheds, where they can roam. These hens wander around a farm during the day, and at night they go into hen houses. Studies have shown that cage-free eggs contain more vitamin A and good fats than cheaper battery-cage eggs. These chemicals are important for a healthy diet.

Free-range hens like these have a more natural life than battery hens.

Good eggs

Eggs have lots of different uses in combining ingredients and making mixtures.

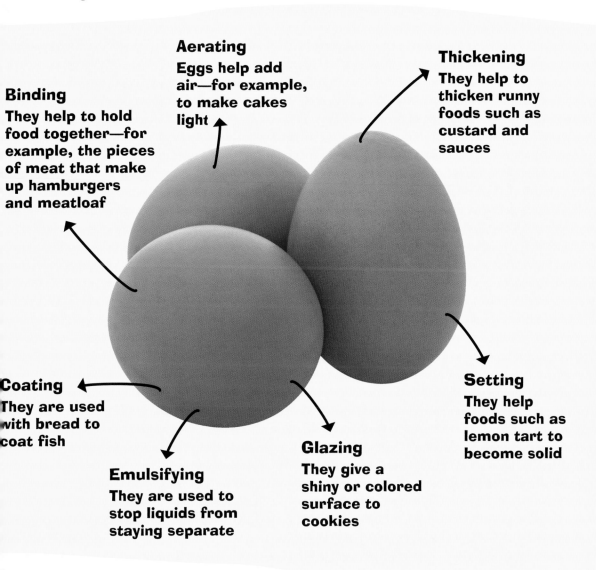

Aerating
Eggs help add air—for example, to make cakes light

Thickening
They help to thicken runny foods such as custard and sauces

Binding
They help to hold food together—for example, the pieces of meat that make up hamburgers and meatloaf

Coating
They are used with bread to coat fish

Emulsifying
They are used to stop liquids from staying separate

Glazing
They give a shiny or colored surface to cookies

Setting
They help foods such as lemon tart to become solid

Always cook eggs thoroughly

Raw eggs may contain *Salmonella* bacteria, which can cause serious food poisoning. Always store eggs in a refrigerator and wash your hands after handling them. Cook eggs thoroughly, so that both the white and yolk are firm. It is best to avoid making mayonnaise yourself. Mayonnaise manufacturers use pasteurized eggs. They heat the eggs at a certain temperature, and the heat kills the bacteria (see page 5).

FOOD SAFETY

Everyone involved in food production must help protect health. We can all do this by using **hygienic** (clean) methods in storing, handling, and preparing food. <u>Bacteria are the main cause of food going bad</u>. Given warmth, moisture, and time, these tiny microorganisms multiply in large numbers in food and water. They cause food poisoning, which affects the stomach and makes sufferers vomit and have diarrhea.

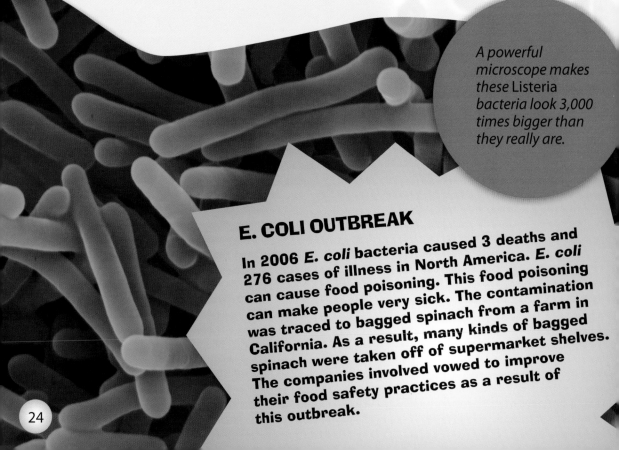

A powerful microscope makes these Listeria bacteria look 3,000 times bigger than they really are.

E. COLI OUTBREAK

In 2006 *E. coli* bacteria caused 3 deaths and 276 cases of illness in North America. *E. coli* can cause food poisoning. This food poisoning can make people very sick. The contamination was traced to bagged spinach from a farm in California. As a result, many kinds of bagged spinach were taken off of supermarket shelves. The companies involved vowed to improve their food safety practices as a result of this outbreak.

Cook food thoroughly

Cooking food thoroughly destroys bacteria. Here are minimum temperatures for cooking meat. Cooks in factories, restaurants, and in the home all need to follow the same rules:

Cuts of beef, veal, lamb	63°C	145°F
Pork, ground beef	71°C	160°F
Chicken and other poultry	74°C	165°F

Stopping the spread of bacteria

Food manufacturers keep all their machines and equipment clean, and they stick to important safety rules. This is because bacteria can spread from one food to another. This can happen easily with meat.

Here are some basic safety rules to follow when handling me

- Store raw meat on the bottom shelf of the refrigerator, so that it doesn't touch or drip onto other foods.

- Wash your hands thoroughly with warm, soapy water after you have touched meat. Keep your fingernails trimmed and clean.

- Dry your hands well using a paper towel or hand dryer.

- Wash chopping boards, knives, tongs, and other utensils in warm, soapy water as soon as possible after use.

- Don't put raw meat next to cooked food on a grill. Otherwise, bacteria could spread before they are destroyed by the heat.

Cooks should always make sure that their work surfaces and equipment are clean.

One in four

Around 76 million people in the United States are affected by food poisoning every year. That means about one in four Americans becomes sick each year.

Using the right equipment

It is important to know how to use the right equipment for preparing and cooking food. For example, the easiest way to check that meat has been cooked through is to use a food thermometer. Most modern food thermometers give a digital read-out of the temperature when they are pushed into the meat and left for a few seconds. There is even a special kind that can be pre-set to pop up when the meat reaches the right temperature.

Electrical appliances

There are lots of electrical devices to help you prepare food efficiently and safely. Here are some of the main ones.

- *Bread machine or bread-maker*: This is made up of a pan, or tin, with a paddle in the middle for mixing dough. It has an oven with a control panel. It can also be used to make pizza dough.

- *Food processor*: This is a machine with interchangeable blades and disks. It is useful for liquidizing soups and making pastry.

- *Hand blender*: This is a hand-held device that helps you mix, whisk, chop, and blend.

- *Juicer*: This is a machine that gets the juice from fruit and vegetables.

- *Microwave*: This is a small oven that cooks or reheats food very quickly (see next page).

This cook is using a food thermometer to check the temperature and make sure the meat is cooked.

BRIGHT IDEA: MICROWAVE

In 1945 a U.S. engineer named Percy Spencer was working with electronic equipment when he noticed that a chocolate bar in his pocket started to melt. He discovered that waves of energy, called microwaves, from the equipment had caused this. Two years later the company he worked for produced the first microwave oven.

Just a little water needs to be added to peas to cook them in a microwave oven.

Good vibrations

How does a microwave oven work? It produces waves of different kinds of energy. High-energy waves called **microwaves** cause small amounts of water in food to vibrate rapidly. The vibrations cause friction (rubbing), which produces heat. This cooks the food.

DESIGNING A DISH

Designing a food product follows three stages:

design brief ➜ market research ➜ design specification.

The design brief explains the need for your product and who it is for. Next, you need to do market research, to find out what people want from the kind of product you are designing. Then, you make your design specification, which is a detailed description of the product.

Design specifications might include:

- size, shape, and weight
- ingredients and quantities
- equipment to be used
- appearance, taste, and texture
- costs.

You could design a delicious drink, like this raspberry and blueberry yogurt smoothie. Then you could give it a name, such as Double Berry Dream.

Sandwich spec

Imagine you are working for a food company. You might design a sandwich. Who is going to be interested in your sandwich—a particular age group? Where and when will it be eaten? Will you make it a rectangle, triangle, or square, or a range of all three? What kind of bread will you specify? There is a wide range of fillings to choose from. You will need to think about the cost of the ingredients, and they will need to go well together. And how will you package and store them to keep them fresh and tasty? There are so many things to consider.

Packaging

Food designers also have to think carefully about how food is stored and packaged. A banana and chocolate sauce sandwich sounds new and fun. But the chocolate sauce might make the bread soggy, which could make the sandwich fall apart. Yuck! A star-shaped sandwich might look nice, but it would be difficult, slow, and expensive to cut. And imagine trying to make a star-shaped sandwich box!

Heston Blumenthal's dish of shellfish and seaweed is called "The Sound of the Sea." You can even eat the pretend sand and sea foam while you listen to a real sea through earphones.

BACON-AND-EGG ICE CREAM!

Chef Heston Blumenthal is famous for studying the chemical processes that go on while food is cooking. He has created some amazing dishes, including bacon-and-egg ice cream. This unusual take on breakfast involves leaving smoked bacon in cold milk overnight. His restaurant customers and reviewers say it is delicious.

How It's Made:
Frozen Pizza

1 Flour, water, yeast, salt, olive oil, and sugar are mixed together to make the pizza dough. Cornmeal may be added for flavor.

2 The mixture is kneaded for several minutes. Then the dough is left to rise.

3 A machine separates the dough into chunks.

4 The chunks are rolled into a flat sheet and given a dusting of flour.

5 Roller spikes pierce holes in the dough.

6 A cutting roller forms the dough into circles, and the next roller removes the leftover pieces.

7 A conveyor belt moves the pizza crusts through a tunnel oven, where they bake for several minutes at more than 200 °C (390 °F).

8 Tomato sauce is brushed onto the crust. Then cheese is sprinkled on.

9 A machine called an applicator adds meats and other toppings.

10 The pizzas are cooled. Then they are put in a freezer for 20 minutes. The temperature inside the freezer is −31.6 °C (−25 °F).

11 A machine covers the frozen pizzas in plastic.

12 Each frozen pizza is pushed into a cardboard box, ready to be delivered to the supermarket.

In this pizza factory, workers add the toppings by hand. They cover their hands, mouth, and hair to be hygienic.

BRIGHT IDEA: PIZZA MARGHERITA

Margherita pizza is made with mozzarella cheese, tomatoes, and basil. The ingredients are said to represent the three colors of the Italian flag (red, white, and green). The pizza was named after Margherita of Savoy, wife of King Umberto I (1844–1900). The Italian queen is said to have visited Naples in 1889 and enjoyed this particular topping.

FAST PRODUCTION

Production companies can control the speed of their machines. At their fastest, cutting and topping machines can produce 180 pizzas every minute.

APPEALING TO CONSUMERS

Manufacturers produce a wide range of foods for today's **consumers** (buyers). This gives people a large choice, from fresh fruits, vegetables, and other raw foods to packaged meals such as lasagna in a box. These packaged meals need very little preparation by the consumer. Food can be bought at many different stores, from small local markets to large out-of-town supermarkets. Modern consumers demand this high level of choice and convenience.

Just like this real supermarket, the online version has a huge range of food products.

ONLINE SHOPPING

Today, you can even shop for food without leaving your home. New technology makes it easy for customers to choose products from a supermarket's website and pay online by credit or debit card. These services are particularly useful for people who find it difficult to get to the store. Online shopping can help fight **pollution** by cutting the number of car journeys made by shoppers.

Sensory testing

Food manufacturers carry out tests to check that consumers are happy with their products. They do this with new products, and you could do the same with new recipes that you create by asking your family and friends. Manufacturers also test existing products, to find ways of improving them and increasing sales. Sensory analysis (how something tastes, feels, smells, and looks) generally concentrates on taste and characteristics such as flavor, texture, and color.

STAR DIAGRAM

Food manufacturers use star diagrams to see what people think of their products. They ask people to rate 8 characteristics on a scale of 1 to 5 (with 5 the highest score), and then connect the dots to see what shape it makes.

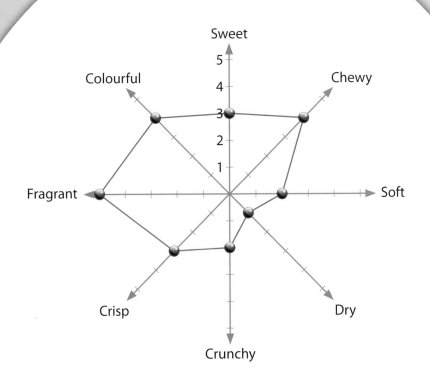

Packaging

Food packaging is used for four main purposes:

- to protect food from damage during storage, transportation, and display
- to preserve food and extend its shelf life
- to describe a product
- to make it attractive to customers.

PACKAGING MATERIALS

This table shows the advantages and disadvantages of using packaging materials.

Material	Advantages	Disadvantages
Paper/cardboard	Easy to print, cheap	Easily damaged, not waterproof
Glass	See-through	Breaks easily, heavy
Plastic	Versatile, lightweight	Not suitable for all foods
Metal	Strong, waterproof	Expensive, not suitable for all foods

Chocolate box packaging looks attractive and protects the chocolates inside from damage.

REUSING AND RECYCLING

Glass, plastic, metal, and paper can all be broken up and recycled, then reused. This saves the energy that would have been used to make new packaging. It also means that manufacturers create less pollution and use smaller amounts of raw materials (natural materials). Recyclable packaging carries symbols that show what it is made of, including the type of plastic.

CAN OPENER FACTS

Tin cans have been used for many years. But they also need to be easy to open. Early cans had to be cut around the top, near the outer edge, with a chisel and hammer!

• The first can opener went on sale in 1858, and it was really just a very strong knife.

• Can openers that used a rotating wheel to cut the metal were introduced in 1870. Their design stayed the same for a long time.

• Pull tabs were first introduced in the 1960s. Today, many cans have stay-on tabs, making it easier to recycle the whole can.

Most drink cans are made of aluminum. This metal can be recycled, including the pull tab.

Modified Atmosphere Packaging

Modified Atmosphere Packaging (MAP) is used to increase the shelf life of foods such as cold meats, smoked fish, cheese, fresh pasta, and salads. MAP works by changing the amounts of gases in the package when the food is wrapped in plastic. This means that bacteria grow more slowly. But some studies have suggested that MAP may remove vitamins from lettuce and other salad leaves. This means it would be less good for you.

What's on the label?

Food manufacturers have to give consumers certain information about their products. The label should include:

- the name and description of the product
- a list of ingredients, including additives (see page 17)
- allergy information (for example, some people are allergic to peanuts and will need to know if the food contains them)
- how the product should be stored (such as in a refrigerator)
- the weight or volume of the contents
- the name and address of the manufacturer
- a "best before" and/or "use by" date
- cooking/heating instructions
- the place of origin of the food (where it comes from).

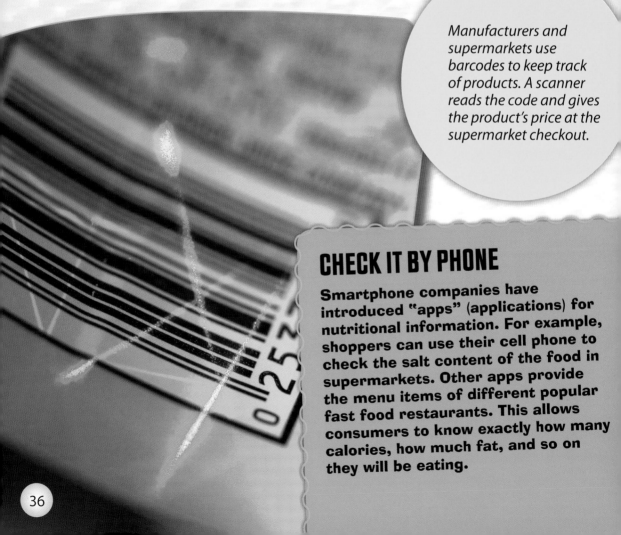

Manufacturers and supermarkets use barcodes to keep track of products. A scanner reads the code and gives the product's price at the supermarket checkout.

CHECK IT BY PHONE

Smartphone companies have introduced "apps" (applications) for nutritional information. For example, shoppers can use their cell phone to check the salt content of the food in supermarkets. Other apps provide the menu items of different popular fast food restaurants. This allows consumers to know exactly how many calories, how much fat, and so on they will be eating.

How do scientists calculate calorie content?

If a manufacturer wants to claim that food has special nutritional or energy value, the label has to give information. This usually includes the amount of energy (in calories or kilojoules) per 100 grams (3½ ounces), or per serving. To figure out this amount, scientists use a measuring device called a bomb calorimeter. <u>Calories are units of heat</u>. In the calorimeter, food is burned in a closed container (called a bomb), and the amount of heat given off is measured. Carbohydrates and proteins produce about 4 calories per gram, and fats produce more than twice as much (about 9 calories per gram).

FAST FOOD AND KIDS

Fast foods are often full of calories, fat, sugar, and salt. In the United States, some people are particularly concerned about children eating too much fast food. Childhood obesity (being very overweight) is a big problem in the United States.

To address this problem, in 2010 San Francisco, California, passed a law. It would make it illegal to provide free toys with fast food meals that contain more than 600 calories, or more than 35 percent of calories from fat. Supporters of the law argued that toys tempt children to eat food that is bad for them. People against the law argued that it is the role of parents to make these choices for their children, not the government.

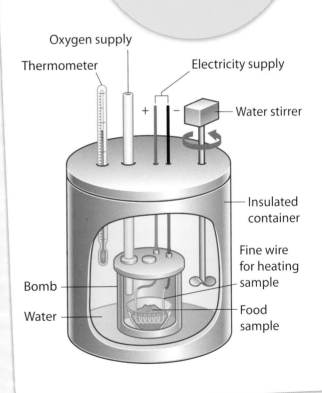

This is a diagram of a bomb calorimeter. It measure the amount of heat a food gives off when it is burned.

Oxygen supply

Thermometer

Electricity supply

+ −

Water stirrer

Insulated container

Fine wire for heating sample

Bomb

Food sample

Water

ADVERTISING

The aim of food advertising is to encourage us to buy particular types and **brands** (makes) of foods. A new brand of strawberry ice cream is more likely to be advertised than fresh strawberries. Canned tomatoes can make manufacturers more money than unpackaged tomatoes.

Many ads are aimed at children and young adults, so some controls are necessary. In the United States, more than 40 percent of food advertising during children's TV programs is for food high in fat, salt, and sugar—such as sweets, soft drinks, and chips.

STYLING FOOD

Food stylists work with photographers to make food look attractive. They have lots of tricks. For a burger ad, for example, the stylist might improve the cooked meat by painting it with oil and brown coloring. For a flame-grilled look, the stylist might make stripes on the burger by marking it with a hot metal skewer.

Modern chefs add style to their food. Their dishes look like works of art.

Space publicity

There is a saying that "all publicity is good publicity." So, is it worth advertising in space? In 2000 a pizza restaurant chain paid $1 million to advertise on the side of a Russian rocket. It blasted off, carrying equipment to the International Space Station. The following year, the pizza company worked with Russian nutritionists and delivered a vacuum-sealed, salami-topped pizza to astronauts aboard the Space Station.

MAKING CLAIMS

Advertisers have to be careful about any claims they make. A large yogurt manufacturer showed many TV commercials claiming that if people ate their brand of yogurt, their digestion would improve. There was no real scientific evidence to back this up, however. The company had to pay a court settlement of $35 million because these claims were false.

FOOD MILES

The distance food travels from where it is grown to where it is eaten can be calculated in "food miles." Food is sent by airplane from one continent to another, and by truck from country to country. <u>In the United States, 15 percent of food is **imported** (brought in) from other countries</u>. A typical prepared meal contains ingredients from at least five other countries. All this transportation uses an enormous amount of energy and causes pollution, adding to **global warming** (the gradual warming of Earth's temperatures).

This ship in Central America is being loaded with vegetables for dinner tables thousands of miles away.

African beans

Despite the problems, some people say food miles are a good thing. When European countries import green beans from Kenya in Africa, the food miles are high. But beans there are grown in a more environmentally friendly way than in many other places. The farms use manual labor (using people instead of diesel-driven machines) and natural fertilizer (instead of oil-based versions). They also give jobs to people in the developing world. Experts say that these beans, even though transported on planes, may produce less pollution overall. This means that they do less harm to the environment.

Seasonal fruits and vegetables

Different fruits and vegetables are in season during certain times of the year. For example, in some parts of the United States, strawberries are in season in spring and summer, but not during fall and winter. Many environmentalists argue that people should learn to only eat the fruits and vegetables that are in season locally. This means food only has to be preserved for a brief time and be transported locally, rather than being sent from other parts of the country or world.

FEEDING THE GREENHOUSE EFFECT

The atmosphere is a layer of gases that stops some of the Sun's rays from reaching Earth. Its gases also stop some heat from escaping from Earth, just as glass traps warmth inside a greenhouse. Food manufacturers are adding to this natural effect by giving off so many waste gases from factories, planes, and trucks. Many of these so-called greenhouse gases—especially carbon dioxide—are adding to global warming.

MEASURING INGREDIENTS

Food scientists use many different measurements. <u>Scientists weigh chemicals and other substances in metric or imperial units.</u> For example, a test tube that measures in metric units might contain 28 grams of a chemical, which is the same as 1 ounce in imperial units.

Cooks list recipe ingredients by weight or volume. In the United States, cooks use the imperial system, which includes units such as cups, teaspoons, tablespoons, and fluid ounces. The cup measurement used for solids is different from that used for liquids. In many other parts of the world, the metric system is used instead for recipes. If you get a recipe from another country, there is a good chance you might have to do some conversions. Here are two examples.

Volumes for liquids

U.S. imperial	U.S. cups	Metric	Spoons
⅕ fl oz. (fluid ounces)		5 ml (milliliters)	1 teaspoon
⅖ fl oz.		10 ml	
½ fl oz.		15 ml	1 tablespoon
2 fl oz.	¼ cup	60 ml	
4 fl oz.	½ cup	120 ml	
8 fl oz.	1 cup	240 ml	
16 fl oz. = 1 pint	2 cups	480 ml	

Weights for flour

U.S. imperial	U.S. cups	Metric
1 oz. (ounce)	¼ cup	30 g (grams)
3 oz.	½ cup	75 g
5 oz.	1 cup	150 g
10 oz.	2 cups	300 g

Quiz

1. How long does it take to pasteurize milk at 72 °C (162 °F)?

a) 15 seconds

b) 15 minutes

c) 15 hours

d) 15 days

2. Which two units measure food energy?

a) grams

b) calories

c) fluid ounces

d) kilojoules

3. Which of these is not a kind of sugar?

a) lactose

b) fructose

c) sweetnose

d) glucose

4. What is the chemical name for vitamin C?

a) folic acid

b) ascorbic acid

c) acetic acid

d) formic acid

5. What is the production process for a single product?

a) batch production

b) mass production

c) continuous-flow production

d) single-item production

6. Which equipment slices food thinly?

a) mandolin

b) guitar

c) banjo

d) violin

7. Who developed frozen foods in 1929?

a) Clarence Seedorf

b) Clarence Birdseye

c) Nicolas Appert

d) Nicolas Anelka

8. When did the first can opener go on sale?

a) 1958

b) 1908

c) 1858

d) 1808

9. What does MAP stand for?

a) modified atmosphere packaging

b) mixed additional packaging

c) mild air packaging

d) mother's apple pie

10. Which instrument measures calories?

a) barometer

b) thermometer

c) odometer

d) calorimeter

1 (a); 2 (b & d); 3 (c); 4 (b); 5 (d); 6 (a); 7 (b); 8 (c); 9 (a); 10 (d).

Answers to the quiz

Glossary

acid solution sour-tasting liquid, such as vinegar

additive chemical that is added to food to improve qualities such as taste or texture

bacteria very tiny organisms. Some bacteria may cause illness in humans.

brand named product or group of products

calorie unit that measures energy in food

carbohydrate starch or sugar in food. Carbohydrates are changed to glucose when we eat them, and glucose provides energy.

carbon dioxide colorless gas that is used in carbonated drinks. Carbon dioxide also plays a role in the environment, as increased levels of it in the atmosphere lead to global warming.

consumer someone who buys goods (such as food) and uses them

contamination when harmful substances, such as bacteria, get into something like food

conveyor belt continuous moving band that moves things along in a production process

developing world poorer countries with less technology than wealthier parts of the world

emulsion mixture of two liquids that will not form a solution (dissolve together)

energy strength and liveliness, and their source in food; also, power that provides light and heat or works machines

environmentalist someone who cares about and acts to protect the environment (our natural world)

fat natural greasy or oily substance found in animals and plants

fiber plant material found in grains and vegetables that is important for health

gene basic unit in living things that passes characteristics from one generation to the next

genetic modification (GM) changing an animal's or plant's basic makeup

global warming warming of Earth's temperatures, believed to be caused by human activities

glucose type of sugar in the blood that provides energy for the body

hazard analysis process to identify potential dangers in food manufacturing

hygienic helping health and preventing disease by being clean

hygienically describes a way of acting that helps health and prevents disease

import bring in food or other items from another country

ingredient substance that makes up part of a food product

irradiation treating food with gamma rays to kill bacteria

laboratory place where scientists carry out experiments and research

macronutrient nutrient that we need a large amount of

manufacturer company or factory that produces finished goods, such as food products

manufacturing process of making something from raw materials

mass production making many of the same thing all at once

micronutrient nutrient that we need a small amount of

microorganism tiny living thing

microwave high-energy waves of energy

mineral substance found naturally in the ground, such as calcium, that is part of a healthy diet

Modified Atmosphere Packaging (MAP) type of packaging that involves changing the amounts of gases in a package when the food is wrapped in plastic. This means that bacteria grow more slowly.

nutrient substance in food that provides nourishment and helps us grow and be healthy

nutritional describing the processes of food that help us grow and be healthy

obesity being very overweight

organic describes a food made without the use of any harmful chemicals

pasteurization process of heating food to kill harmful bacteria

pollution damage to the natural world by harmful substances

preserve keep food from spoiling

protein natural substance in food that we need for strength and growth

pulse edible seeds of crops like beans and peas

saturated fat solid fat such as that found in butter, hard cheese, and bacon

solution mixture formed when one substance dissolves in another

suspension mixture in which a solid is held in a liquid, and may not dissolve unless stirred

Ultra Heat Treatment (UHT) process that heats milk to more than 135 °C (275 °F) for just one second. An unopened carton of milk prepared this way lasts for months.

unsaturated fat liquid fat such as that found in olive oil and other vegetable oils

vitamin chemical that helps us live and grow, that is part of a healthy diet

yeast substance made from a microorganism that is used to raise bread dough and in other food processes

Find Out More

Books

Ballard, Carol, and Neil Morris. *Making Healthy Food Choices* series. Chicago: Heinemann Library, 2007.

Bender, David A. *Dictionary of Food and Nutrition*. New York: Oxford University Press, 2009.

Buller, Laura. *Eyewitness: Food*. New York: Dorling Kindersley, 2005.

Langley, Andrew. *What Do You Think?: Is Organic Food Better?* Chicago: Heinemann Library, 2009.

Morgan, Sally. *Chain Reactions: From DNA to GM Wheat*. Chicago: Heinemann Library, 2007.

Websites

The U.S. Food and Drug Administration focuses on food safety and hygiene:
www.fda.gov

The U.S. Department of Agriculture's "MyPyramid" food pyramid is a guideline for healthy eating:
www.mypyramid.gov

Check out this U.S. Department of Agriculture website for links to a variety of activities and games related to food safety:
www.fsis.usda.gov/food_safety_education/for_kids_&_teens/index.asp

The Fast Food Explorer lets you research the nutritional content of fast food meals:
www.fatcalories.com

Topics to investigate

There are many different topics related to food technology. The websites on page 46 might give some interesting leads. Here are some further research ideas.

Fair trading in the developing world

The Fairtrade Organization helps small farmers in poorer parts of the world by making sure they get a fair price for their produce. In 2010 there were 746 official fairtrade organizations in 58 countries, representing more than 1 million farmers and workers. You could research how this system works.

Multicultural food

Look further at the question of food miles. Consider how long-distance transportation affects communities. Do people in wealthy countries expect to be able to get foods from around the world? Do people from abroad want to eat food from the country they were brought up in? Is food an important part of culture? Do food manufacturers take this into account?

Advertising-speak

Advertisers hope to persuade buyers to choose their product rather than any other product. They use friendly, positive words to describe the products they are promoting. They include words such as *value* or *economy*, *pure* or *natural*, *light* or *lite*. Look at some food advertisements and see if you can find more terms like these. Think about their meaning and whether they help you choose which product to buy.

Index